Minding Our Manners

Saying Please
and Thank You

By Maria Nelson

Gareth Stevens
PUBLISHING

first concepts

Being polite means acting in a way that is respectful of others.

Part of being polite is saying "please" and "thank you."

5

You should say "please" when you ask for something.

If you want your friend to share a toy, say "please" when asking for it.

9

Saying "please" is
a way to show
others kindness.

11

If a friend *does* give you their toy, what do you say then?

13

You should say
"thank you"!

15

That shows you are thankful for what someone has given you.

Saying "thank you" when you are given a gift is polite.

Say "thank you"
when someone does
something nice
for you.

You can always
write a "thank you"
note, too!

23

Please visit our website, www.garethstevens.com. For a free color catalog of all our high-quality books, call toll free 1-800-542-2595 or fax 1-877-542-2596.

Library of Congress Cataloging-in-Publication Data

Nelson, Maria, author.
 Saying please and thank you / Maria Nelson.
     pages cm. — (Minding our manners)
 Includes index.
 ISBN 978-1-4824-1727-2 (pbk.)
 ISBN 978-1-4824-1728-9 (6 pack)
 ISBN 978-1-4824-1726-5 (library binding)
 1. Courtesy—Juvenile literature. 2. Etiquette for children and teenagers. I. Title.
 BJ1857.C5N45 2015
 395.1'22—dc23
                                              2014025644

First Edition

Published in 2015 by
Gareth Stevens Publishing
111 East 14th Street, Suite 349
New York, NY 10003

Copyright © 2015 Gareth Stevens Publishing

Designer: Andrea Davison-Bartolotta
Editor: Kristen Rajczak

Photo credits: Cover, p. 1 Dean Mitchell/Vetta/Getty Images; p. 3 matthewennisphotography/iStock/Thinkstock; p. 5 c12/Shutterstock.com; p. 7 XiXinXing/Thinkstock; p. 9 Fuse/Thinkstock; p. 11 omgimages/iStock/Thinkstock; p. 13 Gladskikh Tatiana/Shutterstock.com; p. 15 Voyagerix/iStock/Thinkstock; p. 17 Andersen Ross/Blend Images/Getty Images; p. 19 Syda Productions/Shutterstock.com; p. 21 bikeriderlondon/Shutterstock.com; p. 23 Sharon Vos-Arnold/Moment Open/Getty Images.

Printed in the United States of America

CPSIA compliance information: Batch #CW15GS: For further information contact Gareth Stevens, New York, New York at 1-800-542-2595.